T0150855

THE EIGHTH MOUNTAIN POETRY PRIZE

THE EIGHTH MOUNTAIN POETRY PRIZE was established in 1988 in honor of the poets whose words envision and sustain the feminist movement, and in recognition of the major role played by women poets in creating the literature of their time. Women poets world-wide are invited to participate. One manuscript is selected each year by a poet of national reputation. Publication and an advance of one thousand dollars are funded by a private donor. *Cultivating Excess* was selected by Judy Grahn to be the 1991 winner of the Eighth Mountain Poetry Prize.

1989
The Eating Hill
Karen Mitchell
SELECTED BY AUDRE LORDE

1990
Fear of Subways
Maureen Seaton
SELECTED BY MARILYN HACKER

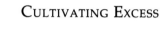

CULTIVATING EXCESS

CULTIVATING
EXCESS

Lori Anderson

THE EIGHTH MOUNTAIN PRESS
PORTLAND · OREGON · 1992

Grateful acknowledgment is made for permission to quote from:
   The Selected Poems by A.R. Ammons, copyright © 1977. Reprinted
by permission of W. W. Norton & Company.
   "Bells in Winter" and "The View" from *Bells in Winter* by Czeslaw
Milosz, copyright © 1974, 1977, 1978 by Czeslaw Milosz. Reprinted
by permission of The Ecco Press.
   Gravity and Grace by Simone Weil, copyright renewed © 1980 by
G. P. Putnam's Sons. Reprinted by permission of The Putnam Pub-
lishing Group.
   "Sarah's Choice" from *Sarah's Choice* by Eleanor Wilner, copyright
© 1989. Reprinted by permission of the author and The University
of Chicago Press.

Cover art by Angelina Marino, used by permission of the artist
Cover design by Marcia Barrentine
Book design by Ruth Gundle

First American Edition, 1992
2   3   4   5   6   7   8   9
Printed in the United States

LIBRARY OF CONGRESS
CATALOGING-IN-PUBLICATION DATA
Anderson, Lori, 1958-
      Cultivating excess / Lori Anderson. —1st American ed.
          p.   cm.
      ISBN 0-933377-18-5 : $9.95. — ISBN 0-933377-19-3 : $18.95
      I. Title.
      PS3551.N37446C8   1992
      811'.54—dc20   92-3104

The Eighth Mountain Press
624 Southeast 29th Avenue
Portland, Oregon 97214
(503) 233-3936

ACKNOWLEDGMENTS

"On the Last Page of Her Diary She Said She Was Two Severed Selves" was published in *Denver Quarterly*; "Coming Home Older" was published in *Iowa Journal Of Literary Studies*; "Brutal Said: Mysticism Said: Merge," "How I Fell in Love at the Herbert Hoover Museum," "Sacrileash," and "Under-Hymn" were published in *The Little Magazine*; "My Thin-Sliced Agate Heart, Cracked and Copper-wired to a Black Belt Sings" and "Losing My Lucky Nickel at a Reenactment of Custer's Last Stand" were published in *Seeds: The Biannual Literary Journal of The Sisters of Color*; "Adhering" was published in *Sing Heavenly Muse!*; "Dead-I," "Grave Stones Dressed as Isis," "Rock Scolds Stone," and "Self Portrait Eye to Eye with Clinometer & Prism" were published in *Walking The Dead* (Heaven Bone Press, 1991); "Adding to My Angelhair Collection," "Autobiography," "If This Quilt Were Made of Fire," "I'm Talking Fast to My Sister on How to Sharpen an Ax," "Ode," "What If I Write a Poem in Which a Mammiform Situla Speaks" and "What Then" were published in *13th Moon*.

A reader familiar with the poetry of Deborah Digges, Jane Miller, Jorie Graham and Judith Johnson may see and feel the presence of these gifted teachers in my work. I certainly do. I am indebted to them and to the community of women whose poems fill my life. *Cultivating Excess* was created in conversation with the visions and voices of Mary Ellen Ionas, Jane Ann Fuller, Sheila Griffin, Sheila O'Connor, Jill Hanifan, Tess Lecuyer, Nancy Klepsch, Sharon Stenson, Darby Penny, Epi Cintrón, Druis Beasely-Knowles, Roz Lee, Wilma Kahn, Suzette Bishop, Jan Ramjerdi, Amy Schoch, Katie Yates, Cindy Parrish, Lâle Davidson, Beth Weatherby and Carla Steinberg. Who could do it with fewer friends?

for Jill

CONTENTS

II. SILVICULTURE

III. CIVILCULTURE

IV. EXCESS ISIS

I. Excess Jesus

Under-Hymn

Sunday slips down like a snapped panty mid-cheek
for picnics/ Prayer partners pack a snack/ Grace in the grass
bare-assed behind sumac/ How great thou art how great

Heaven is laden with harlots and hoaxes/ And none of us
ever wanted stigmata/ nails or not/ just a hot
Sunday slipping down like a snapped panty mid-cheek

The semen-aryan's trigger finger eases on in the choir
girl after girl/ dear wretches god saved like me
bare-assed behind sumac/ How great thou art/ How great

Somedays this congregation just sucks/ Blonds bad-mouthing
sodomy wives and the whole lot/ all the while wanting
Sunday to slip down like a snapped panty mid-week

Semen says/ the dick's daddy's/ baby/ belongs in
the pulpit/ Your chickadee throat belongs in the high loft
bare-assed under choir robes/ How great thou art how great

So we girls stuck smut under steeple struts
let our own hands go roving right under our hems
let Sunday slip down like a snapped panty mid-cheek
bare-assed on high/ How great thou art/ How great

What Then

If ladies, not angels, came & emptied
the tomb — rock at the door their labor

If He was dead on his back in a boat, craft
built for men (the women in a hell oaring)

If Marys unshored him, rowed him to sea
where he had failed what his John taught

If head underwater is head in spirit
& we never walk on flesh but through, waves

If neither weak nor dead weight, we indeed
in faith's manger lay down as angels cannot

Fish in Air

You & I — new
    lovers at Eagle Something
        Park in a WPA tower
where I play princess-
    held-captive a 1000 stone steps
        above a river 5 miles wide
at this mouth & you don't even
    look for eagles & long after

      when sufficient-
ly horrified
    at how woman you are,
        you gather a holy host
of others (your Father, your Friends)
    male trinity ensuring we
        only look for eagles. You all
agree on one I cannot
    see then tell a tale:

      7-foot sturgeon flailing
so much that the eagle could not
    fly nor take back her talons.
        Down, down they both drown —
consequence of coveting says
    the father as he gives you
        binocs to be certain you see.

But how else would eagle ever enter
      water to such depths save
            by an anchor of flesh? Maybe
her longing is as ours is:
      fish in air, bird under
            water, man off earth (woman in
heaven) ((heaven down under))
      flesh needing flesh to rise
            to delve to depths beyond/above
our allotted home.

      You & a new
            lover eagle at your something
tower\where she plays
      Captive?
            1000 steps above water
wide & wild at your mouth

Dead - I

"If I only knew how to disappear, there would be perfect
union of love between God and the earth I tread, the sea I
hear."
                                                    —Simone Weil

The landscape lacked nothing except Simone Wheel
(she be ideal, she be idea, she be I-dead)
lacked nothing save perhaps a sax.
So, in whimsy, I hiked her back. Baby
this here is Buck Mt. — one big riff between
God's earth & God's water. I tried not to be

flippant, but...she be
dead-I, she be invented-I. Weil,
explain this: union is between
God & _____. Earth-I is deadly?
Put your hand here: feel my beating, my breathing. Baby,
you didn't really want to live with so little sex —

little syllogisms your sax.
At the summit, when waterscapes began being
a full skirt about us, I turned to name a baby
pond, her very clit, to make her wheel.
She disappeared. Who was I to disturb the deadness,
the roar of heaven/earth, the union between

creator/creation between idea/I-dead between
the rift the rift? Oh that iphigenial sax
sucks. I tinwhistled "I-deal-dead-
I" all the way down to a motorboat being

11

revved-up. I begged to be a water wheel
buoyant like in a dreamsong that babies.

Last night, I got Bulgarian women with bambinos
singing a bandito-I-I-I-I, a harmony between
sleep and wake, distortion disappearing like Weil.
I was smug and keenly aware of sex.
My walk had a wiggle the way I wanted Weil to be—
so her authority, her annihilation would lose its deadening

pull on me. Weil, I will not be saxoned
into scalding my feet or forgetting to eat.
Between the sea-I-hear & the girls-I-kiss, my sax
and me sing: If a genie, I owe I owe. If be genie, I owe.
B-B-B-Baby

Coming Home Older

I. Diorama (Salt Lake City)

I, tourist, would push this button forever
to keep the angel lit

If America's Joseph, this Smith, would stop
his spectacles, his reciting

of visions. I want you not the man
to talk, turn neon,

tell me my mission, o beauteous
angel of wax. I've followed

the blue books of Mormons
all the way from the land of Junípero Serra

motel by motel, and it's too far
not to have seen inside

your Temple — tower, spire, silent trumpet
held by a golden herald. Must I linger here,

visitor citing brochures
in chorus with Joseph?

Can't you let me in?
I just wanted to touch your ear,

tell you of my home, of the fountain
at Mission San Juan Bautista. There's a flea market,

a monk's robe, eucalyptus leaves.
I could adorn you

with the waters and wonders of this world.
You could give me wings.

II. King's Highway (San Juan Bautista)

No lord, child, just thirst.
Thirsting and quenching

& quenched spirit's no good — that's why
we work toward always wanting.

Kingdom *at,* never *in,*
hand. Going for the bush

just to feel
birds ignite into flight —

the harder, the sweeter. The liquor
we all drink:

words mostly, pretending
we can fly.

When we can't, pillage…
missions, towns, this market

stall in the heart of El Camino Real.
Go ahead, buy it.

Hat from fragile feathers of a white egret
worn by a lady between wars.

Go on, St. Paul said cover your head
so as not to tempt

angels, meaning men.
See how they turn

& with this hat — long, exquisite plume,
finest of waterfowl —

you could begin your quenching,
could learn your loveliness.

Cottonmouth

Some sassy girl dares me
to lift the lid, to outright
look in, maybe even rummage.
"We can necklace the lewd parts."

      Cottonmouth,
      maybe you a whole snake again,
      maybe when the man cracked
      you a whip to stone, you swallowed
      venom, maybe it waits bait —
      each livered piece luring.

Still she says go, says I
was the last in the water, says I
owe it to the hand on the dock
who pulled me out.

      I swear snake,
      I never saw you, didn't know
      they'd shovel you out, trash you up —

           (I was just lily-floating away:
           today I learned when to call water a wake,
           when to let loose the tow, glide
           into sleepy water.)

That girl said you wanted your head
in my mouth, said I wanted it too —
me belly-up and hogging the whole lake.

I swear snake,
I never saw you. Just that hand
hollering for my hand — it wasn't
my mama who docked me, it wasn't
my papa who shoveled you ashore.

> (I knew nobody, and no body was talking
> as he did what he did. 'Cept this girl
> reminding me how luck is.)

Stone

Who are you creeping
    in my pew like a ma
like a pa? I know when
    to rise. I sing on
cue. I got my fingers
    holding the right
hymns.

Your looking at my
    looking is blocking
my views of holy up high.
    I've seen the real
light making stain glow.
    Up there we hang
angel robes, end choiring.
    Don't need god-ghosts/
grown-ups when we sing.

    You gonna stop
that man last Sunday
    who was poking his head
out side doors, messing
    with me, making me
call my dad to make sure
    he comes gets me.

He comes. I tell you.
    It ain't nothing
to waiting cause he comes.
    You all messing
my hopscotch making this
    stone in my hand heavy.

Rock Scolds Stone

I. Stone

Read your book.
I, pietà, never held my dead son.
Mic just rolled back marble
in my lap. A trap.

Get this boy's body off me.
How? The way you got Joseph's.
Call your angel-thieves. Body off me,
body on me. Never once a word
from me. Angels always taking over:

Holy, Holy, King, King, King.

I was a heaving woman in labor
& angels hollered holy, holy, holy
so wisemen would find it satisfactory.
His weight in me like this eternal

dead weight on me. Pushing, Pushing.

I want Joseph most of all. Because
then the pushing was pleasure.
Then when I said my god, my god
it was for Joseph's second coming.

I see Joseph in every crowd.

He is the face of all of you.
Ten in ten tourists are him. But
that day in Jerusalem, no Joseph.
They crowned and crossed our son!

Good God, you could have at least given me

Joseph. To make each day bearable,
I make this stone-son-of-mine
Joseph. Joseph living and in
my arms. I invite him into my soul.

Joseph has become my holy ghost.

If I gave up Joseph as my cross
to bear, didn't let lust lord
over me, called this stone "Jesus"
would this body rise up off me?

II. Rock

I, the rock of Sisyphus, say: Stone her.
She has forgotten Michelangelo.
Each day his hands on her. His hands here,
then a thigh, here a face. From his hands
a whole body, then again a whole body born.
Both reflective, emotive. All earth's motion
stilled in a moment she embodies — the eve
of redemption grounding our grief for once.

Does she want to be rolled by Sisyphus?
False caresses at the base of the hill,
coaxing me, as if a cry could change
Hades. Half way up, it's really hell:
the same goddamn confession. Palms feigning
prayer. His breath foul self pity.
At the top, he's pure fist, pounding out
failure then pounding out pure fear.

Last of all, most of all, Your Highness,
Your Holiness, you are rockness. Regardless
of the story, you are rock — testimony
of our planet, molten at the core of its own accord.
Forget the story, forget Joseph. You are rock:
molten at the core of your own accord.
I, I am not even a real rock.
Without the story, I am nothing. With the story,
heave-ho, I am everything that burdens.

Brutal Said: Mysticism Said: Merge Naked Self Said: HA!

"I dream of a hard and brutal mysticism in which the
naked self merges with a non-human world and yet
somehow survives still intact, individual, separate.
Paradox and bedrock."
                              —Edward Abbey

        Dear Dead Abbey,

Who said "Here fishy-fishy"?
    Boy leash-walking dead fish:
Who said "You in need of a dog"?
    Girl high on her hot rock:
Who said "HA!" to cool pool,
    to small circle, to simple song's
sweet "Please Touch"? Is that what fish said?

    "From here, Fishy, your decay is
undetectable. From here, man, I love
    you." What do you say

I keep you at bay. Hate
    to see that boy rope you up
drag your bones with a ripcord
    from his bedroll, drag your body
in small circles with simple song.
    That's what rock said.

Dear Dead Abbey,

Who said "Ready to address excess, sir"?
     Boy petting headless plaster hound:
Who said "Yes, shark art howls, ma'am"?
     Girl guarding plastic bone heap:
Who said "AH! to decapitation,
     to the sweet AWWW OUUU within"?
Is that what head said? "Tease the jaw

     that won't snarl: Honey, can I
touch your skin, prettier than metal
     amaryllis." Is that what tourist said?

Guarded art's guard: Hate
     to see you spiral down
museum's scheduled spiral song,
     spiral down the "Don't Touch" —
Victrola hound without a head.
     That's what flesh said.

Sacrileash

There is this leash from light
    and blood to some of us
                unheld
    taut and unheld

There is this leash, call it
    desert and want of well
              being
    sing on, sing on

There is this leash w/in me I
    held one dawn, left earth
              tethered
    lead on, lead on

& 7 days after the trek, when leashes were fashioned, all roamed
over the high rocks, that every would-be leash would be brought
forth

& when these were ushered here, when each had come to be a leash
& gathered where we are, at dusk we strung them together; you too
strung them together

& when leashes had been braided, then these were oiled & softened
into reins — short ones, very short & thin — very thin

& when night invaded the young then galloped about Boy-Who-
Walks-

The-Dead; we-including-you harnessed him with miles
of leashes; we-including-you wound leashes upon his limbs

& after him, we-including-you, strung, knotted & hung rows & rows
of all kinds of leashes, the most gorgeous leashes, the thinnest
shortest leashes

then leashes were offered to all the others-who-walk-the-dead;
they were yoked with reins; they were radiant with reins, leashes
were wound round our-including-your limbs here in high places.

& when midnight came, we-including-you nayed (neighed?) & took
to cantor (canter?) fiercely in syncopation we-including-them
galloped.

We-including-them leash deflowering.
     We-including-them leash empowering.
          We-including-them leash petty cowering.
          We-including-them leash lashing.
leash leashing extending short,
     thin, oiled reins
          reins & reins of
               leashes we-including-you leash
something precious like smell like heat
     like house. We-including-you rein
          begetting and beguiling.
          We-including-you rein
injunction & instruction. We-including-you rein
     into one place out of one hand.
          Out of one place into one hand
               & the dead walk with us

Ode

Truly she was a live one this dead one
Truly alive one dead still one being
one exalted more a dead living one
one sitting always one being her back to the view
Truly dead one always one accused of being
jabbering mutton tender button back to the view
struggling truly to be meaning how one is one
always expressing living jabbering dead living
as live tender buttons glisten listening

Most truly she wanted to be great this dead
one in paris making americans her back
to the war never jabbering about dead ones
Her being as a live one this dead one one
exalting the living and their being repeating
as expressing living repeating struggles to be
always a jabbering american dead listening

Exegesis and Her Song

"Let us formulate it thus:

        yes, the Universal is
devouring the Particular… and each day
we ourselves lose letter after letter from our
names which still distinguish us from each other."

        If I proclaimed this
particular Milosz loudly at 11,000 feet
called San Luis to a gaggle proclaiming
their right to Looie

        cause they're right
of continental divide arrogant in accumulation
of vowels oblivious to original stark consonance
of sacred omissions in the name of a god they've come
to make personal as if they could distinguish
themselves,
        I did not succeed.
For secretly I too had thought I had risen
above certain christians camped below
baptizing in our leeching field. If
need for water, any water, makes my waste
holy in such a particular way that I must
devour myself, I confess:

I deny it, gather letter
after letter changing my name from son to song
as if I had been trod on down into this world
and could dance the fragments of my steps back,
as if close in my bones

I hear the tremor
a great water wall waged here crawling grey
moraine calling over south slope's dead spruce
zone offering offering steps dear stones.
Scree and scream:

I add another letter.
Stutter *er* is her and so much more moves here.
Hear it: Anderson, Andersong, And Her Song...

II. Silviculture

Day 124

Bailey's boot grease warmed on the back burner.
My fingers dipped into the hot belly of the can —
anointed, then taken first to the black tongue
that bears the wounds of restraint, of laces taut
to keep the boot from being swallowed
by mud of a forest in which it might rather stay
(more so there with mosses than in a closet,
more so than on my foot walking it to sure death).
O that these moments in hand would be enough
to mend with mink oil the scars of misstepping.
I'd end this, bed you down in a soft bog
if not for work and want of woods to walk.
But you are not without recourse, you hard heel.

Self Portrait Eye to Eye with Clinometer & Prism

1.

First, Prism said, you must know you are good are sampled are
counted only if you are severed and not entirely detached.

Also, you must always account for slope always maintain proper
distance from higher ground. Oh Clinometer, help.

2.

So look, she said this is the severed tree we're in it has three
legs we must keep on the third it is a day's work.

Unaided eye, I'm brought along with her the other the privileged
whose gift is altered focus she keeps fractured by subtle turns.

3.

Oh but you can learn with her, Clinometer said, numbering in
degrees the depth the deepening ravine the bedrock the taproot
water lap you measure by feel by fall. With me she tilts Prism to
my number severs creation so the detached is easy to dismiss —
whole flowerings scattered in one big loves-me-not. Simple.

You can't see her do this, can you. Your own body blocks you
a small bridge where a third eye should have been. I am I assure
you a third of a sort. I am I assure you trustworthy.

4.

Meanwhile she parallels me for a necessary traverse a brief
transit I've been looking forward to all day. Trees about us no
longer commodities our body taking us for ride — bed rock water
lap. Periphery a polka, certainty whole and multifold: berm grove
vine. As eyes we are unable to look away we see we see.

5.

She goes down on Prism. I pay the price we owe when she wants to
play when she takes to the maze of calculated angles leaving me
to grey miles blurred or stray objects tempting me to forget
necessary distinctions. The optic telling me I see what she sees
telling me I'm needed in her seeing. I sleep on the lie, a
conscious costly sleep absent for the tally one log two log four

Can I blame the hand that takes it to her?

6.

If she gives it up, if hand hands prism over, untrained-I-I
stutter, I get a denser duller fuller forest panorama not fractal
fractured well-formed excision. Wh-Wh-Where are you? She can no
more come to my aid than gut, ear or any other organ & if she
herself sees, it is lost on me. A voice calls out "lazy."

7.

This is it. This is what annoys me she finally speaks choosing
herself to be with me in the dark of my monologue. This is it:
that you think that we could be should be equal voices. Do you
want that we be eyes on different heads with songs like bird

beaks? Our power is in great optic: we focus it distinguishes we fracture it names. These are waking hours. Your joy you think secret and slanderously free from refraction and calibration is not. The neurodance is neither yours nor mine.

8.

After her scold we go about our task as always I mutter underbreath mine mine mine dear eye dear eye

Berm

So Mister Forester when we're done with every berm,
        grove and vine on this goddamn compass line,
we're taking the nearest deer trail to the road. It's
        gonna be two & a half miles uphill in the sun,
        no trees, yes sir.
You ever see a deer with a compass? What animal would
        walk straight through a grove of devilsclub
save one who gets a paycheck? Mister, you can't
        pay me enough to listen to any more of your
        machete-chattering.
You chop down one more bush I could have walked around,
        and I'm heading for the rig.
This "weak-legged-woman-with-no-woodsense" is trying
        real hard not to like you enough to inflict
        some real physical pain.
I want to get you out of this underbrush and walk fast,
        faster than you ever.
Something about this pre-sale timber cruising eats
        the kind part out of a heart.
Something about the almost lover-like gesture of
        slipping one's arms round a tree at breast height
makes me want to see you sweat, gasp for air, pretend
        you aren't hurting.
And don't think I can't walk fast enough. It's just
        that in here I can't seem to touch any more trees
        with this embrace.

Reclaiming Slashburns

I've trapped the Von Trapps
into silvicultural lessons
as perverse revenge for film-
screen's escape-made-prance
(fa-la-la-la-lalalalala)

"How far up
did trees used to grow?
How much tundra
did you sing to death,
kids?" Of course, I hated

how they outnumbered me
in hope and ignorance. I wanted
to lose them
on non-alpine slopes. Teach 'em 2-4-D
& slashburn.

"That there is logging
trash. What voice
would you give hills here?"
Precious windpipes
smoke-raw, they didn't say much

on their first burn, stood dumb
with their shovels, crowded close
on the fireline between ash
and green. "Hey,
I said be lucky

you didn't have to pick-axe
this perimeter.
Your safety is someone else's
sweat." I was being mean
'cause I was a misguided youth,
you know the kind

with the romantic education:
watch a film, carry a tune
then happy ending,
happy ending. I was holding them responsible
the way I can

in my imagination any old day.
Burn #2 was supposed to be an honor
I assured them: "The torch
crew one step
ahead of the smoke,

backs turned
from damage in a quick getaway."
I can speak with authority
cause I have
lain in a ditch dead

tired, 200 acres burning
at my back — 150
to go. Me and the guys singing
nothing, saying
nothing, coaxing our grip-hands

open
with our free
hands, the ones that refuse the torch
but remain indicted by the bodies'
unison and the paychecks' purchase
power. The Von Trapps

here in reenactment, really,
to give voice
to the hell I couldn't sing then.
Hey Isis, goddess of severed selves,
of lost members, of child/kings left

in hell, join us. If we believe
you are with us, help us
reenter the land I prepared
for 2-4-D. Pre-replanting, these chemicals leached
down into the water

where women drank and bred
and miscarried. The names of children
chosen but unused, conjured
perhaps on Sunday hikes
through stand after stand of same crop trees,
the names of a non-merchantable

species equally ghosts.
Our hope tonight is a reclamation of fertility:
the land's, the women's, the wounded
psyche's. Isis,
if you ever worked, work for us

tonight as we move by body
memory alone through thickets as practice
at letting nature take its course
at surviving without ceilings
without chandeliers of incandescence.

In the understory under stars, I need
forgiveness from the 200-year fire
whose cycle my torch has interrupted
so I can sing along with my entrapment: Dear habitat,
my edelweiss, "may you bloom and grow, bloom...."

"Dominance Potential: A Useful but Still Crude Concept" for Insuring Survival of Intolerant Species

Wanna manipu-
late me predict-
ably? Use DP.
Wanna pre-empt
what I got? DP.
Still crude
concept just-
ifying 2-4-D &
T in Nam &
forestry. DP =
[(Pr)(Pe)(Pm)]G.
How big you
want? Multiply

our prob-
ability (Pr) of surviving
resource deficiency (any
will do, cut job
training, cut child-
care, cut education,
medical aid, adequate
housing) times

our prob-
ability (Pe) of extinction
by predators (a little
war on drugs, a little

war with scuds, coup
flu & infiltration) times

   our prob-
ability (Pm) of miscellaneous
disasters (AIDS or acquaintance
rape or pan am or pan pest-
icides) times

   a target
population by outlawing
abortion by sterilizing by job
discrimination by gay
bashing by deportation by color-
coded incarceration.

ONCE YOU GOT IT ALL
plugged in, intensify it
by GNP. You too small
to play w/ Big Intolerants?
Take DP to your bed,
to your dinner platter, your
little front yard or gutter.
Wherever your hands or
mouth work. You can.
Like here: how I did it
in rant. Now I got my DP.

I'm Talking Fast to My Sister on How to Sharpen an Axe

Finger the blade
till tongues curl.
File to that edge
to that recoil:
long, slow — take
its scars. I show
her just right. Good.

       Here, finger first its blade.
       Now heave-ho & axe.
       I'm talking fast: Sister
       save the sweet grass & planting!

Angle, pressure,
stroke. I show her
stance, backcut.
Then we begin
to bring it down.

       Go. Heave-ho & axe.
       Lost: a hillside & a half —
       our sweet grass & planting.
       Only once does she say we are mad.

Manzanita after
manzanita, laurel
arbutus too:
we're clearing
a fire lane. Pray:
dirt eat fire.

      Lost: a hillside & a half.
      Maybe we are birds rebuilding;
      only once does she say we are.
      She swears a bit, maybe at smoke.

Pray: no more
ash. Wind's a hiss,
far ridge's begun
to char. She sings
conjuring canoes.

      Maybe our birds are rebuilding.
      The ridge has begun to char. She sings,
      she swears a bit, maybe at smoke.
      The wind's a hiss and fast.

Portage after
portage: squat canyons
to cool pools.
She sings the arc
of us. I remember.

Ridge has begun to char. Sing!
Take manzanita & laurel too.
The wind's a hiss & not too far.
Begin. Arbutus after arbutus.

She swears at smoke
maybe at birds
rebuilding. Never once
does she say we
are lost. We drag
slash to far fields.

Take manzanita & laurel too.
The rhythm, the swing, we
begin. Arbutus after arbutus.
She's good. I mirror her backcut.

Still with berries,
she calls the way
easy. We save
each other that way.

Her rhythm, her swing. Then we…
she's showing me just right.
She's good. I mirror the backcut.
Slow, even…plant it hard.

We plan sweet grass
and planting. We lie,
we work off that lie.
She's talking fast: Sister.

She's showing me just right.
Note what you want then long
slow, even...plant it hard.
Try double force. Bed its blade.

Prescribed Burning

I. The Fire Coursing From Across

salal & slash
said I pity
   you and fusing beyond
said you
   are merely fuel which I
consume yet not
   withholding
honor.

So, "My dear
moxie" began
   my letter home
"how it was
   that...then
fire came coursing
   'cross
from _____.
   _____ formed
seething."

Mom wrote
back: "ever since
   the big bang
worked its way into
   the universal

shouldn't we all
    just be simple
flint schooled
    in the match?"

    Indeed. There's
sweetness in
    the aftermath
digging through
    lazy ash.
Clanking our shovel-
    heads together.
Singing: "in
    the flame our
cadence is."

II. The Dragons Coursing from Within

Making my bitter brush
bite the dust
fire said
you suspect I'm
the cause of
forces within your control
& I'm going to chide you for it
I said
go ahead

Those hot spots these sulfur pots
fire said
are dragons in petty bargains
I hear you I said listen to yourself
we too are deaf dragons

Frankly fire said I'm
everything vital
temper temper
cooling volatile with vile

Those are my words
I said
fire claimed
fair exchange

Deaf on hot sand I
turned bought my ground
with volitant steps
tender altercations

To Keep Our House Whole

Chief Enright or warden
      whatever hatchets the head
            off, sifts
sawdust in his hand saying:
      yes, this is
            what gutted that
house, such a small
      doll will gut it all.

Mom asks if
      the body burns.
            He says safe
& slow, so he bags it
      to go, praises
            us: brave & big
for bringing her, leaving
      her head here.

      "Mama, don't
gimme that sack,
      don't say you can
            sew a head back."

No big-girl would hide
    the beheaded
      in a bag, the brave
would hold it on her
    lap & chat: o cheer
      up, we can still have
tea, I'll tip
    the cup, somehow
      you'll drink it up.

Scaffolding for Conflagration

Barn, body or some suitable effigy ignites & a lady flails
but ultimately up-&-walks-away — boards The Train

To Elsewhere. We cry: "Run, Bambi, run."
Someone should drown too. Child as log.

In a pond under a trestle. (Same train?)
& we're never the body that burns (we're always the child down

& under) so we heap kindling hot.
& a stranger sees it, a stranger we're made to want to meet.

& because I want a subplot autonomous from us, I shall be
a black, black ladder-back with the ubiquitous presence of a cat.

& I, chair, shall speak in the voices of those who sit on me.
& the order of all who come should be important.

& the stranger is always first and last (the promise of paradox).
But our lady never sits in the chair (never embodies me).

Yet her child calls it arbor & crawls in (caging the-kid-within).
So in the end, it (I & child) will be the effigy after all?

The battle will be the not relinquishing to or the compulsion
toward the blackness of that ladder-back, the likeness of it (me)

to your own spininess. Because somehow it (I) harbors us (you)
from X, or is a harbinger of X, the X that forces a story once

again and again upon time, the X I want named more than the lady,
more even than the child — the forest within.

So, the stranger (via seemingly fine sex) embodies X?
The one hand whose clapping sounds the whole understory's

mourning for the lone tree heart's hatchet fell comes?
Hardly an answer for any reversible mistake at our birth.

Baby, we best burn this and begin again.

III. Civilculture

If this Quilt of Names Were Made of Fire

If this were made of fire, each panel
eternal, inferno through which we pass
safely, how many candles in how many
windows would testify: "See. I have loved.
Love, I am loving."? How many in how many?

Because this is not stone, not immovable,
not exorbitant freight weighing us down, not
an historical past. Because this is not bronze,
not a cast assembled for hegemony,
we can find its fabric water, enter a sea
with its names claim: "we've all bathed here
and must walk away changed." Some already have

been born again. Taken new names, breathing
among us waiting to see what was learned.
If the handiwork that summons us pleases us,
we succeed in our grieving and have already
unveiled a plan for piecing ourselves whole.
The weave, waves. Our hands, oars. Navigation
charted, as always, by the shape-changers.

Shape Changes/Shape Changer

Call it a poetic conceit, sweet fantasy,
but I will still believe some have been born
again. Stan was still sleeping in this bed
when in the bed across the hall Ariana was
conceived. Stan was still sleeping in this bed
when Ariana came within her mother across the hall
asking, "Do you need more pillows, more food,
more love? Call us family. We'll call your family

when you want us to." When they called
the family, Ariana was still in the womb.
Stan is no longer sleeping. In his bed,
I wake, cross the hall, hold Ariana,
ask, "Do you need more milk, more clothes,
more love?" You'll let me say I was
holding her for Stan, but will you let me
say I was holding the Stan in her? As guest

I was an usher for this young family.
I wake from Stan's bed to take them today
back into the French Quarter, the first time
since the last time they went into the Quarter,
but first we hold photos of Stan and Ariana-in-
Ariana's mother's belly in the French Quarter.
The last photo they had. And when in the Quarter,

lost, they swore they were looking for a Bistro,
but I know they were looking for Stan. They were
angry, each knowing another place to find him,
each seeing him somewhere else, each holding

Ariana, saying you should see her Stan. I smiled
for the photo, holding Ariana, knowing Stan

somehow. And when the storm came and the shop-
keeper kicked us out, I got the taxi to stop
but not quite close enough, some Stan-in-me
took charge. Knowing they were out of the rain
but were not safe, Stan pulled the plastic back,
pulled rain cover from Ariana's mouth and nose.
How long had the air been cut off like that?

That is not a toy. This is not a game, pulling
the plastic back from the suffocating child,
asking the man in bed if he wants more.
Do I make Stan less of the man he was by my saying
he is here now, teaching us at every turn
in the way we care for our children, in the way
we work for their survival, in the way we
recognize ourselves as family beyond blood?

On the Last Page of Her Diary She Said She Was Two Severed Selves

Anne Frank takes
    to the ice in gold-medal
        Hamill-camels because it pleases
me. Damn the ease
    of it. Her here
        perfect
without practice, without
    hours on the ice — an angel
        come for roses.
Me making
    no mention of the attic.

In-the-attic-Anne was
    body.
        This one's book, read
illicitly after
    hours under covers
        by flashlight. My fears:
merely father and
    the possibility of
        rattlers underfoot.
I want to grow up. But why
    keep putting her back in
        the attic?

On-the-ice-Anne beckons:
    we could

skate together, centrifugally
at the velocity of a circular
    saw blade, cut through, sink
        with the stage, emerge
sufis —
    synchronized.
        Pink swim caps our
turbans. We could
    warm this
        frozen river.

I tap my
    toe on the crusted
        snow, don't move
from my bench. I used to
    tour with an Israeli
        troupe, love Al
Tira the best — "Be Not
    Afraid." Feet in wide
        stride, arms swing
freely with
    the body. Look
        left, look right, leap
low and stretched. Then
    straighten — this is a dance
        of
strength.

We performed
    barefoot at seders in aqua
        dress. Once upon a
rolled-out marly
    floor, twice upon a
        cement slab…never

on ice, never
    a risk of falling
        though. The best few
were Jews. The rest
    merely eager.

Anne, a girl named
    Gordon, Judy
        Gordon taught me to
waltz — perfect
    counterforce, 180-degree
        turns. Eyes stead on
the immovable, imaginary
    center-
        point and the bodies
whirling double
    dervish. And without
        music. We couldn't do
that Anne.

If I came out on
    that ice, at best
        it would hold
me. I'd pause where
    you are, see you
        elsewhere — on
the trestle or back
    on my bench. That pole,
        center-ice, would be
white as anywhere. I'd cross
    completely to
        the sycamore, walk
the bank and take
    the bridge home.

Eating Soup by the TV Everyone
Was Saying I Was Caroline

Living in a de-moc-ra-cy
           we took turns
                      a-s-s-a-s-s-i-n-a-t-i-n-g
John F. Ken-ne-dy.
           We prac-ticed his dy-ing
                      on the side board
of my 2nd uncle's
           old Model T.
                  I, Ruby, turned
shot my brother
           Oswald,
                      who swoop-groaned
where my cou-sin
           J.F.K. had just come back
                  as Ruby
who shot me
           who was Oswald
                  who shot my brother
who was Ken-ne-dy.
           We just kept kill-ing.

Tom Sawyer's Island (Disneyland '67)

How come there's no Huckleberry Finn?
This place is crawling with Delaware Minutemen.
Bluecoats with muskets to keep us on trail.

Not me and my brother, we slink behind trees.
Now I'm calling to the mainland: "Quick come,
the dumb tyke's lost and brush is thick."

Dad comes on the ferry looking less like Lincoln,
more madlike — and Injun Jim with a quick belt.
I'm to wait at the gate for word.

Then comes this man being Robert E. Lee,
asking my name as if he's got a secret
pistol in his boot so I tell him: Lori Jo.

I follow to this clearing circled by Mounties
whose horses neigh because the wind is
like before a scream. There comes another.

A Crockett in a cooncoat, bearing knives, lies
between his teeth, saying he's seen my brother
on a horse, with a man, riding like he's John Wilkes

Booth just come from killing Lincoln. I yell:
"My brother's six, and the kid can't kill.
My dad's roaming these woods even if Lincoln ain't."

Petrified, the words don't come.
Crockett, closing in, curses girls lax in mothering
who slink off trail letting loose of father's sons

among armed men. "He's six and the kid can't kill."
My voice gets him thrust from a Mountie's horse.
Clung to my waist, he screams toward the gate to shore.

Losing My Lucky Nickel at a
Reenactment of Custer's Last Stand

It's 20 minutes till Cavalry comes, so I go
in search of popcorn. A man in war paint stops me
at the first tepee, extends his hand as if to ask
for money. I offer my popcorn quarter. He frowns.
I empty my pockets — offer jacks and a ball.
He frowns. Out of my shoe, I fetch the Buffalo
nickel I've had since my third birthday. He nods.
I press it in the center of his palm. He takes me
inside his tepee, sits me on a pickle barrel.
At a checkerboard, he tells me I will be red.
A bugle blows. He centers his fist, forefinger
saying he is Custer. I counter, mirror his move
all thumbs. Ignore the squares, he says, circle edges
keep your ear to earth, let hooves tell you when.

Sure it's a lie. Maybe an eager child could stumble
innocently in. I thronged with all white-born ringside
begging to see the erected sacred for a day to two. But,
how could I lose that nickel? I was too shy to put it in
his pocket. 20 minutes outside of Fargo, crowded bus
helping us share. Too sober, I took his hand off my leg
too soon. Unhooked our held hands too quick. Scared
ever so slightly, I could have waited it out. Got down.
God knows I've paid a higher price for other strangers.
Maybe he knew why we re-ride exact paths with wrong words.

Harmonica

edits us. The refined overdefined our fathered
learning making roads and minimalls of our flesh
which we are too true to

tanned calves of cheerleaders pom-pom our way
in astro turf we water buttonhook gameplan rooted
nuclear and targeted by young boys

who wouldn't venture 'cross churchside nutrition
munitions guardrail I cannot court this winter
of desert vigil prayer of trafficked praising

the lackadaisical sweet swearing of veterans
the enlightened PSAs the ribboned trees defoliate
the mobile storage the fragmented subject cannot

backlight a practiced screw for stage without
discord our blue guitar hurts its cause and hungers
the beast in our cells offering the benign

who boasts the stench of consent
as if fed beside the hooves of livestock sow
owing no one and abandoned on bad land we know not

in which treaties never hold as evidence
with our own hands raised another Roosevelt
any president infertile cone of pine-away prayers

to whom give garnish give fetish give gunnel fire
to whom the multi-quivered arrow bow bowl borscht
for our gut for our gall our biceps the recoil

You Better Remember Your Own Immunization

On immunization day
in Daddy's gymnasium
Daddy says: Here,
catch this, throws
me a medicine ball
too big for me.
I fall, we laugh.
Daddy says I am
a good girl 'cause
I lined up, drank
vaccines right up
from the paper cup
like a good girl.
Here catch this,
he throws me
a medicine ball —
a game we play
as my reward.
See he's got a key
to some back room,
to the medicine
balls. The game
catch makes a girl
strong. I fall,
we laugh in Daddy's
gymnasium on my first
immunization day.

It was a premonition.
Now I see:
my whole generation
has been thrown
a medicine ball too big.
None of us are immune:
we'll all get knocked
down, our immune
systems knocked down
sooner than later
mass tragedy
a pharmacogenic man-
slaughter. They took
the risk-takers first.
Your mama warned you
they'd take the risk-
takers first. Now
healthy with harmless
HIV handed death
prognoses via AZT
poisoning — a medicine
ball too big. We all get

knocked down. You think
you're immune because
you're not named
hemo or homo or
addict or African,
but honey you've had
your antibiotics,
your food additives
your home herbicides

your workplace pest-
icides. Your target
group maybe pre-fixed
heterosex yuppie, but
baby you're acquiring
among your possessions
immune deficiency
cause generations
have been conditioned
thrown a medicine
ball too big.
You and your x-ray
vision ought to
be able to see
we've all been fucked.
In Daddy's gymnasium
nobody's immune
unless you mean latin
immunis as in exempted
from service, from duty,
as in exempted from life.

You better remember
your own immunization,
you better act up now,
you better stop massive
propaganda of AZT for T-4
counts below 500 & hyper
HIV hypotheses. Change
your risk taking, risk
educating your mother,
protest profit making
off your brother.

Investigate the fraud:
shut out AZT-lymphoma
and homophobia. Don't play
with Daddy's medicine.
There's only so much abuse
any human body should
take from corporate
government's medical
specialists, especially you
women. We women are
the fastest growing
population dying from AIDS.
And when AIDS is renamed
to include her symptoms
with his, even more will be
dead. By the time it's
renamed so you too can claim
medical aid, even more
will have died. Bugger your
government till it spends
more on AIDS research.
Needle your government till
its scientists understand
how they're screwing with our
immunity. Inoculate 'em now.

Adhering

Why were we paying a para-psychic $66 to ask us if our mothers'
    uteri felt like soggy nerf balls?
A. said the living room suddenly smelled like turkey dressing, said
    that part of her conception was warm, but that she balked —
    floated for hours before attaching to the lining.
G. said she smelled nothing, probably because her mother hadn't
    come.
If you must know, I adhered willingly, such has been my life.
But if anybody ever asks me again about going down the Fallopian
    tube, I'll say I felt like Patty Duke in a prom dress descending the
    stairs, that all the sperm at the landing had faces of men, even
    women, who've made a fool of me without force.
I'd ask him/them right then to guess whose face is glowing
    brightest.

Autobiography

about being born and always breathing:
always a promise about being none other
until house begets house begets house

for my being here always keeps me asking.
The owners and their "whys"…same story
when I wake too: "It's not your house."

When I know my way, I go to the next house
that feels good, but when I go to my house,
it's not my house. Why do I feel good?

For I know my way: I am always fleeing
in a residential area. Therein is the bed
in which I dream: so returned to my allotted.

When my level could not rise, I saw no more
measured growth by the height of my eyes. Mirror-
stalled, I go to the bathroom, watch myself.

Doubly-cross, I cross the street, still no other
me. Perfect promise for a doppelgänger, but
lawn-walk-gutter-street-gutter-walk…

An Elephant's Rollerskate's Dreambook's Opening Entries

1.

I am human & invited
to play volleyball with good women.
The beast in the barn across the alley shakes
the edifice, bloats up like a blowfish
demands immediate release.
I say that can't be an elephant.
They assure me it is & escort me
to a man-made lake for adolescence.
30 little dumbos practice their strokes
synchronized in a swim to shame otters.
I rejoice for a beast generation in new motion.
They dampen me with news of a toxic waste virus.
As a human, I am indicted.

2.

It's a Cousteau underwater angle:
scissorkicking elephant legs. I'm
trainer for life riding piggyback whole hog.
We're guiding timber down warm pyre-water.
For once, baby, I'm singing River Ganges
oblivious in my buoyancy, thinking
friction's only metal rolling
on circus cement — tons pressuring me.
Waterlogged, I'm sure
my bearings will never be balled up again.

It's a sweet death, Ellie. Submarining
between severed mahogany on TV.
Then the sinking feeling: hell's this
same circuit from Toronto to Calgary.

3.

I wake to vowed to collusion. I got to
persuade these obedient machines,
got to stop our revolution.

Ars Poetica for Halloween at QE2 Open Mike

I. How Many Calories Are There, Dear Data, in 'Droid Dreck?

"I am not less worthy than Lore. I am not less."
Said the second son, the less human son of Sun-King.
The holy Dr. Cyberneticist ships out for the last time
as his evil son kicks his head in, singing a daddy-done-
me-wrong song, kicks his head right in. Riker to

the rescue. Boo. Hiss. We've seen this birth-right-rot
before. Data in a heap on the floor. "I am not less."
Perfect. Our hypothesis pans out. Golden Star Fleet serves
heavenly hegemony as another Jacob gets his justice.
And we weep: *Ha, Ha.* Reconciliation. Propitiation.

Let's slow this warp speed down to supper time.
Let's look at our own dinner table. Here, on planet Gaia
the guy across the table's marked himself as Math.
I'm his sister Lor-i. Literally, culturally we got paths
that cross only at Christmas. See, he can say to Daddy:

logarithm, logarithm. I can say to daddy: lyric, lyric.
Daddy can call our gravy a Heraclitean river, but
it's clear cholesterol through the gut of us all.
Mother knows cause she still skims (centuries later)
fat from broth, still cooks blood from beasts.

My point is nothing discernible: caloric heat of the rant,
heat of the weep. You tell me how to step out
of the oedipal, out of the twin cycle. Electra what?
Tell me how to step out of the womb not less perfect, not less
worthy, not less human. Those who will handle me institution-

ally may watch Star Trek nightly but they will not think of me.
Only of their own homing devices and miscalculations, as I
now do to you — ignoring the mythos of your slick costumes,
ignoring your need for useful data, for singable tunes, for
parental substitutes, for cosmic victories won at warp speed.

If I fail you, disassemble me. Touch my innermost, audience.
How will you know when you find it? With what rhetorical tools
do you hear here? Android ear you've been programed for a hot bar
maid who is salt and sass, whose clarity is hallmark like Happy
Humpday, Happy Humpday. In deepest sympathy, bon voyage love.

All I've got is 'droid dreck: printout after printout verbalized
with an ear to alliteration. Pin-balled between particulars
input by pop-culture and academe, academe and dream. So what
if I take 5, 10 minutes from you. What if transmigration, what
if soul is an accumulation of such encounters with orphan song?

II. Deanna Troi Translates

Though invention, he is human
because human inventors invest him in human drama.

He is human because he is a she
in costume here tonight for you. Check the eyes:

they are not yellow. Because of the stage lights
she cannot see you. So, this is not conversation:

this is not anything really, save an act.
A kind of communication by pace by intonation.

What do you hear? Hot, fast, big words
small heart? She doesn't know how to play the role,

how to get rid of her own voice, how to claim
her own family from the mythic

cycles she can only dully name. Not because she is
a dimwit. Because it has become such a mess

by this century, technology so primitive
in its understanding of language, of hope,

of whatever, I suppose. What else
is she supposed to do. Her homework? She's rigged it

so this is her homework, her happenstance
her halloween. Can you blame her?

Can you blame yourself, waiting there
for your own turn, up here at the helm. What alien

will you scold, what joke will you hopelessly try
to get? What kind of galactic team will you join?

Free enterprise? Captain, oh my captain,
is not every ship in this sky pirate?

How Many Sea Men Does It Take to Screw a Light Bulb?

"Such is the subtle elasticity of the organ I treat
of, that whether wielded in sport, or in earnest,
or in anger, whateverthe mood it be in, its
flexions are invariably marked by exceeding
grace. Therein no fairy's arm can transcend it."
—Melville in/on/thru *Moby Dick*

1.

"I have an idea,"
     sang Isaac to
          Ishmael. Watts was
here in Calvin's
     stead, tuned-out & fed
          up with re-hemming
holy cloaks of pseudo-
     sacrificial do-dah. "Ha,"
          said the narrator
privy to sea-worn
     semen-aryan pulpits
          (damn retractable
rope). The twin I's monkey-
     groping Pegleg and Queequeg
          up an escalator to
NY State's ex-
     hibition of Names
          Quilt because American
imperials provide for
     AIDS as Ishmael

       allows for resurrec-
tion/insurrection-erection
      of others in his own
         fictive one. God,
who is dead, knows.

         2.

Not quite a tour-
      ist in any para-
         digm, Ahab got
coaxed into cement
      prow of an edi/ori
         fice, bowel hull
in which state
      workers shall feed.
         Ishmael did it.
Buggered Ahab's ear:
      "If this quilt were
         water, one big Möbius
dick folding back on
      itself like the comforter
         on your very
bed, well then these
      names are the Elect,
         pre-graced — death by
sperm whale, needle whale,
      hegemony the beautiful."

3.

Wanting his dick
    remembered, knowing it
        couldn't be so hung,
Ahab, kick-ass up
    the Möbius stairs to
        claim his stake
braggin' his whale big-
    ger than Pliny's: "If
        I ever go where
Pliny is, I, a whale-
    man (more that he
        was), will make bold
to tell him so" was what
    he planned to say, but
        as it happens, the
Quilt silenced even
    the least who went first.

4.

What's a him-seer
    for my dear Watt-
        song? The narrator's
flippancy supposed-
    ly buoyancy, like
        a TV-dolphin-sit-com,
was meant to stop
    Isaac from surveying all
        the quilted sea as
sorrow and love mingled
    down some wondrous

wretched cross between
pity and sin. "Alleluia?
        Alleluia?" Ishmael
        wept out of Isaac's
reach. Until Queequeg's
        hand found a panel
        whose alphabet he was
certain was not a name,
        more a symbol like
        his own mark. Holy
Unsaid held forth
        & taught. Yojo his crown
        chakra because all
are opened by this.

        5.

Who'd have thought
        Ahab would have
        succumbed to Gnostics.
Squatted on his hams
        by the Black man & cap-
        tain-preached the secret:
The Kingdom of God was
        before them, and after
        six days Jesus told
the youth to come
        with linen and naked
        body to remain the night
for mysteries — boy with
        boy. Jesus & his John
        having a whale
of a time. When I ask

you, will we bless
    our priests for this
very goodness. A whole
    parish made this
        panel by which Quee-
queg taught us to
    pray. Oh Ishmael!

    6.

    Ambushed!
The coins of Noah,
    the dinnerless student,
        all of Aristotle & Quail
fueling national arm-
    ada. Queequeg deemed
        nobler fodder. Gnostics
of no help. Canon-
    ical performance: "free
        will had received
a mortal wound." Pre-
    destined innocence pre-
        empting death as un-
merited. Miracle
    made General of all
        particular ground
tactics. Commercial time
    more frequent, the names
        of the dead with-
held. The homos to be
    kicked out after they're
        killed. Continuous

convoy — the intest-
    ine of a leviathan
        that surely eats me.

    7.

Because I am not
    Ishmael but am Ishmael
        more so than Isaac,
I am frightened
    despite the savior
        coffin. If I see
AIDS as high speed
    replication, the virus
        strains. But if rapid
risking is immune
    system's breakdown,
        time shifts fear.
But if fear of writing-
    time became for-
        mulated: to add
letter after letter
    in pronounceable se-
        quence need not happen
faster than our losing
    letter after letter
        from our names as if
what once distin-
    quished us, always
        does, even after.
Then. Wisdom
    Wisdom = Horror Horr-

or. The The.
   "Unity cannot do"
      the particular any.
         Measure by
measure. Music?
   Mostly.

      8.

Plot time: it is
   time for direction.
      All to be lost
at sea, save Ishmael
   whose biblical id-
      entity entitles
him to bob back
   in yet another
      story. So let A-
hab and Quee float
   in grief's reverie
      because I want
Ishmael and Isaac
   to kiss and make out
      here among time-
less lovers. Heal-
   ing as "Sarah's
      Choice" demands
(a Wilner poem
   I read aloud)
      "'But Ishmael,'
said Isaac, 'how
   shall I greet

him?' 'As you
greet yourself,' she
        said, 'when you bend
            over the well to
draw water and see
    your image not
        knowing it reversed.'"
A = not A.
    That is plot,
        timed by choice.
In revision Sarah
    must harbor Hagar.
        Each woman ceasing
as obedient
    wife of a God-
        chosen Abraham
to sanction in lust
    Israel and Egypt bedded
        together, their sons &
the nations they be-
    came, coming out
        as lovers, spooning
in the former gulf.

IV. Excess Isis

Meditation as/in Isis

I use Isis for power. In this,
I am like those who used her before.
The image, per se, of Isis tall and winged,
guarding a small boy Osiris is no less
my protector than, say, the Isis shrunk in wedlock
without her wings tending a dead king, searching
wherever the hell she goes for his missing
member. Nonetheless, I have my preference.

Proportion pans out more, more often
than not: there is more milk in the big glass.
The small tumbler leaves me thirsty — a state
or sensation for which I have no single image
only a sticky dryness which slows my speech
to a stutter, to a choice between gr-gr-greed
and n-n-n-need. The shared ease of speech prefixed.

And if, because of the absence of either Isis
image on TV or billboards, I carry inside me two
i's and s's in a sequence that intensifies
being by its double meaning and musical
repetition (as in mama), then perhaps, I tap
a ground that is more electrical than earthen —
more an arbitrary zero of potential than a chosen
ballast of, say, homeland. My talking this way makes you
dizzy, doesn't it? Leaves you longing for simple

story: in a time other than our time, once
there was this king, this queen, something dead, and
something never quite dead that reminds you of your
self. "Before that?" you ask. Then after all that,
you ask: "Who is the Isis-in-you?" And my eyes
stare straight ahead, see you, light bouncing back
hitting the same nerve you always do, flipped
several times as optics demand. Blind thinking
charging us, again — conspicuous circuit is-is, is-is.

Grave Stones Dressed as Isis

The earth is cut out for remembering our dead.
Why shouldn't it take all of us?

Cliffside, we leave the monk's hut, take libation's
cup full breast. Our odds on flesh

to outcast stone, we finger slivers of relief
simply modeled with a rasp. We

follow mantle fringe, hover where chisel claws
shallow, where tunics knot, wanting

our own contours traced full breast, simply with a rasp.
Wanting to know the slow stone rattle

to usher dead girls into dance, our odds on flesh
we work stone wicker baskets to empty

mysteries left uncarved. As if sacred objects
couldn't be trusted with dreaming

girls, the curious locals drink us in as exotic.
Say our motives are confused.

Say the goddess hides behind our uses.
For her we're here with no other

chores. Save to celebrate mother's milk. Save
to free the body's swing. The earth is cut

out for our remembering. Why shouldn't we
gather a book full of names. Why?

Adding to My Angel-hair Collection

I'm giving mama's 75 Santas crewcuts today, trimming their beards
to look like daddy's. Somebody's got to unify role models dining
here. I'll sweep up the scalp-scraps with Oral B wizardry as a
thank-you-dear-hygienist-of-the-home for feeding, cleaning and
filling my rotten sweet tooth. Thank you for the gag of "Please
Pass The Salt."

& when the Clone-Hos look like insurance salesmen they might in
past lives have been, I'll beg them: depreciate mama. Take my
hot-headed heart, a chip off her stoneware. I'm reckless as a
dishwasher. As a daughter, I'm one of many chances she has to cry
herself to sleep, to decorate her home. My hair, then, is always
important. The hair of those-who-hold-me is not as important as,
say, their genitals. I assure you, mama,

she is sweeter than we should talk about. So Ho-Ho-Ho. Here's
another Santa for your collection. I had wanted, this Christmas,
to give you something other, say, the zippers from all the
presidents' wives' dresses. Who in West Branch, Iowa would miss
them? Herbert Hoover is 8-ft under his own museum & Isis is a
lousy sentinel. Who will blame brazen bronze for coaxing the
skirt off Jackie O, for ripping the zip right out.

Isis, I'd instruct her, my half-sister is a headless bodice with
well-proportioned hips who lives with 1,000 thimbles in my ex-
bedroom. Queen of the rick-rack, this white-gowned manikin is
mama's voodoo cushion. These days she's making jewels of ancient

needles. We're trying to cut down on the ouch between us. We could, I'm sure, open up more with first ladies to practice on.

What I'm trying to ask you Isis-I-saw-In-Iowa is how liberated were you during the great grave relief rubbings? There in Greece when some dissertation made it her business to undress your stone likenesses with a caress of granite's fabric knot between your breasts, what did we gain? Can I give it as a gift? If I take a woman in my arms, rub a soft circle right here, will it warm mama as angels cannot?

How I Fell in Love at the Herbert Hoover Museum

I tried battle chat over ships drydocked in miniature: "Yar,
what hell hull." I admired defloured relief sacks poppied
with Belgian crewel work, let the guide set Hoover's birth cradle
rocking, then abandoned my summer beau to the presidents' wives'
dresses to stand forthright in front of an un-interred metal Isis.
She'd be the next dead god I'd marry. "Goddess," she'd correct me.

I was dressing her in Jackie's inaugural gown, trying Eleanor's
pumps, liking the mismatch, wondering what happens when Isis is
manikin. Clark Kent can fly and his underbelly is cruciform.
If under us were the dress of Isis, maybe when the call came
we could transfigure, could shed journalistic disguise, could,
could…what? I asked the cute wisp who borrowed my camera.

As happens when plot must advance, she happened to be going
to Greece, happened to need a companion who owned a Nikon,
happened to think my new shoes were her size. We would go to
Attica. We would document all the girls who donned the dress
of Isis. That's the way she said it. I loved the tangent:
its occupation with dress not goddess, with movement in stone
not in neo-ritual. "Keeps distances safe." Safe from what?

My mother collects Santas, lines our hutch with them so you see
I'm trained to love a hand going to its icon repeatedly
instead of to me. A Santa once told my mama she was a good girl.
Now she gathers a choir to remind her. What my lover wants

from girls dressed as Isis, I can't say, but tracing mammiform
situlae stone after stone to get a feel for illusion as motion
is a song her hand brings to me nightly. It is not a choir,
not first ladies loose from pomp-&-pumps of their biggest ball.
It's more. Like a child's first mastery of safety pins —
release and attachment, finally, without the prick.

What If I Write a Poem in Which a Mammiform Situla Speaks

& the first line says suck me
& the second line says suck me
& the third line senses your saturation but says suck me
so as to impress upon you
the goddess's likenesses in me & mine
in you & yours the uses of milk the same
as before myth & mouth interchangeable
cows sacred because of calcium
& the tingle in your bones when the bite comes

How I Fell in Love…Waiting

We screwed, we slept, we woke, she kept dressing, so I sang
"Counting Cowdays": "Once the Von Trapps were dressed in
curtains & each was given a hoop & scythe, the hills came alive
with so-so, fa-fa, do-do, do-do — calculating carrying capacity
blues. Children ringed grass, clipped it clean, multiplied
its heft times X per hectare. If cows, they could eat for 70
days, counting Maria, always counting Maria. Moo-moo, Baa-Baa."
She begged: "Shut up and put down the drapery! Am I, am I
dressed okay?" Jackie O might have said no, but "Love," I said,
"this, your fifth outfit, is as lovely as I am blue-ball bored."

She acted all Marilyn Monroe, so I got more foul-mouthed.
To watch her re-dress I took as an honor, as re-invitation too.
The 'gasm to outfit ratio inordinately top-heavy, so unlike us.
While coming, she said to me: why? why the Von Trapps? "So song
will save us dear." Then sing, she said, doing another riff
with her forefingers she called Mama's Power Stone III & IV.
I wanted more of course, but she rose and donned a mourning suit.

"How does one dress to greet the geezer who carved your mother's
gravestone? How does one explain the need to hear the chink-
chink of a particular chisel?" How could I answer her?
She was taking me, I thought, to a backalley rockshop
where electronic drills spell the names of newly dead. I got
a stone city where white roads quarried marble for dance halls.
Many men stood amid stacks of slabs deadening us single-handedly
with the steady, dull clack-clack or work ethic's chip-chip away.
Two out of seven were carving names of dead. The rest: US flags.

She said we could bed this chosen chisel rhythm, keep it going
for the transatlantic long-haul. I didn't want chisels, only her
words over and over. The underbelly of the hill ripe with echo:
men's blasting block after block still howled the long haul from
hole to light. My nightmare was being trapped far from any Isis,
immersed in the cadence of old glory carved in American bedrock -
a cadence not even an unfurled ancient goddess could dub.
When do we go to Greece? She said shhhhhh & you'll be there.
I didn't believe but I heard myself say Yes. Yes, Isis, Isis....

"Did I think," she asked, "a good ferryman should
warn his heavy load of architectural abomination in case,
for example, some stone is dreaming of marking a First Lady's
bones?" Was I supposed to answer a question like that?
I assured her a democratic majority of bedrock knows nothing
of the dress of Isis, but it was a fool earth that didn't want
to necklace her breasts. She said yes, yes, Isis, Isis.....

Fixated again on her, I shopped for jewels in my head till
she said what stones does your mother wear on her neck?
What millstone did she hang on yours? Mother, oh my mother:
She who curses exchange of toil's sweat for fine dress,
she whose wrist is steady as the neck of an axe,
she who counts only downbeats of luck, wears shards of wit
and a servant's heart. She strung me with Santa's ho-ho-ho's,
a toybag and elfin tools, saying: "Get to work! What are you
waiting for?" Laughing, my lover said my heart was uranium.

Curtains and Cowdays Explicated

Julie Andrews, as Maria, did dress
the kids in curtains — green trees
on alpine white. In one night,
which I think is funny
and implausible, the singing
ex-nun-nanny made eight
outfits perfect, letting the sun
light and war trounce in the once veiled
windows as if clothing
ourselves in what once secluded
us, saves us.
My mother was the best seam-
stress in our extended family,
and she'd have needed many
nights for one little lederhosen.
The movie did not
do justice to the process of fitting
a picky child who prided her-
self, as I did, on sabotage.
Mom's mighty competency invited
the devilish in me
to dance. So, there
you have it: I was
sitting safe in peace-
time privilege in no need,
really, of a filmscreen
nanny. Mother was
far from dead; Mother was
my very sparring
ground. The feisty survive

so mother must create
fighters: coax and coach, prod
and depride. Let the dog
bite, let the bee
sting. Make these your
favorites. Such counters
the cowday-concept — a kind
of cowardice, a false
calculation, like Andrews'
songs. Carrying capacity
is taught as a handy
forecast for how much
grazing any hill can
give assuming one cow's
eating's the same as
the next, assuming each
square foot of dirt grows
equal grass. An old joke: justice.
To assume makes an ass
of you and me. The basic
question answered at the onset:
no, we cannot all
eat forever? *So*, to plop
the ill-fittedness of curtains
and cowdays mid-lesbian-lovestory
means what to what reader?
Would a woman who loves
women conjure Scarlet's defrocking
homestead's velveteen green
so as to win a Rhett?
Hardly. Crossdressers
want the veil torn
want the dirt: how many
fingers, how flat
the tongue? How long
do you want bedtime,

how far is the nearest
convent, did the neighbors'
children sing along:
Honey, Honey, Lord, Lord.
Was anyone watching?
How deep into
the next war were we?

How I Fell in Love...Shopping

Things were missing, of course: Mrs. Clause, that Osiris thang,
the baby (cradle left rocking), ritual instruction for suckling
mother's milk wrist-whisked about in brass breast cups by Greek
girls wanting little to do with Iphigenia. So, we went shopping.
"How is it," she asked, "you think I need more?" Gunsteel —
a minute bead had brought us to a halt. I hated it, ogling
the incremental. I bought in excess. She acted shackled.
If she were to wear runes about her wrists, she wanted old ones.

The diamond stud in the clerk's goldplated nail sang: Be right
with you dear. Diamond coaxed gunsteel from a velvet pouch
whose fabric's psalm thanked Master Merchant for not having
made them prom dresses or bearers of an Elvis crotch shot.
The clerk was good. "An ex-purse that carried gold between wars."
She said something about a deep poke within. My lover dipped
a dirty fingernail in the metal lily's stamen: the bead scene
swirled meteor through black velvet lava. Breaking the consumer

rule: no alchemy with merchandise pre-sale. Tax and tip
mandatory unless of course you court the clerk. The flirt
infuriated me. Good God, Mother of Isis, I mean, Isis-Mother-Of-
All, save me, shop for me. She came, dangling from Flirt's ears—
two Egyptian coins worth less as tender. In bartering, I found
the story of who we were and what we did rendered them ours

for good. From that ritual forth (that girl giving girl sacred
tokens), the Von Trapps' promise (safety in Vermont) bored me.
In each graveyard catalogued, I took to making altars. How do I
explain this: in leaving random objects, objects not predicted,
not dictated as missing pieces to past political puzzles, I
imagine that these quiet, private particulars whisper power
to my hand directly. Let me touch your face. Let me show you.

My Thin-Sliced Agate Heart, Cracked and Copper-Wired to a Black Belt Sings

Never take a gift-belt in your teeth
like a horse bridled — your neighs nayed
by a mama's giddy-up girl yanking your mane
reason for becoming being jumping her barb
wired corralled-in heart her mama fenced up
like a Dakota poor farm by dust by dung.
Chaff from her mama's mama's milking hands
spooning in potato mash then shoving soap
to wash the foul out. Cry ouch ouch
and bite the hand that won't feed you
song. Say hey diddle diddle. Demand cat,
demand fiddle. Say: my gut's a rock heart
she wired me with. My song's a black reminder
of the whap whap for the sass back and soul talk.
My weeping's for a mother having to be told
so long. You've been a child so long.

How I Fell in Love...Undermining

The moment of the balk — what tarot koan would that be
(reversed sound of one hand cupping) when girl-at-altar-asked
to-hand-over-the-next-gift-to-a-semi-randomly-selected-Isis-dress
can't lay down Graceland: her pen in which an Elvis head cruises
the pink Cadillac forced across America's acropolis? An Icarus,
a failed Isis with wings, doomed because his head isn't throned?
Questions enlarge when you call your gifts to stone-girls kitsch.

This week's graveyard had blossomed with locals: olive branches,
a kind of azalea, evil-eyes quietly accumulated on my altar
as women came to watch my lover be the anthropologist of Isis.
I fancied myself as the tourist/priestess, collected stories:
one said her sister ran off with a Yugoslav who juggles pianos
with his feet (would I like to see the video?); one wanted
courage not to name her first daughter after her husband's
mother. All suggested we vacate the premises by Easter. Why?

I'd have stayed firm & planted if not for Graceland in hand &
a big balk in my heart. I needed more: hieroglyphs? homecooking?
What in hell was I doing, what? Did you ever memorize a monologue
your lover used to explain your *litost* away? "The earth is
cut out for remembering our dead. Why shouldn't it take us all?
Wanting to know the slow stone rattle that ushers dead girls
into dance, our odds on flesh, we work stone wicker baskets
to empty mysteries uncarved deep. Odds on flesh to outcast...."

In tuning her out, I knew my new project: the Isis/Santa ratio.
A merging of math and pictoglyph, perhaps as a murder mystery.
Maybe this was my chance to blame Martin Luther's reformation
for all First Ladies. Once committed, the oracle overtook me.
Some island's omphalos asked me what made Crater Grail a cup,
silly chalice for holy knights? "I am not a navel," she said.
And I had to admit my belly flowers lower at the power stone:
no woman would trade clit for phallus by choice. Ask Pythia.

Egyptian Greeks liked temple sleep: Incubatio bought future,
brought dreams to those who laid on graves. Magic turned oracle-
seekers to pliant priestesses. Poured out like blood like sheep,
I too saw in afternoon heat a light fixture I was convinced was
once a lady, knowing: This is the order of life. First earth,
then mouth, then form. For stick begat fish begat monkey begat
me. I dress in the colors of blood, night and sea and I dream
of becoming a wheel, an orb — of becoming becoming a catapult.

Notes

Dead-I
"The landscape lacked nothing except" is from Czeslaw Milosz's
"The View" from *Bells In Winter*. (New York: Ecco, 1978) p. 12. The
Simone Weil epigraph is from *Gravity and Grace*. (London: Ark, 1987)
p. 37.

Brutal Said:
The Edward Abbey assertion that provokes this poem is from *Desert
Solitaire: A Season In The Wilderness*. (New York: Simon and Schuster,
1991) p. 6.

Sacrileash
This poem borrows its ritual structure from the Aztec festival "Offer-
ing Flowers" in Jerome Rothenberg's *Technicians Of The Sacred*.
(Berkeley: University of California Press, 1985).

Self Portrait
This poem follows Jorie Graham's mode of "Self Portrait as _____
and _____" found in many poems in *The End Of Beauty*. (New
York: Ecco, 1987).

Dominance Potential
"Dominance Potential: A Useful But Still Crude Concept" is the title
on a class handout I received while studying silvicultural practices.
DP "is the relative ability for a species to pre-empt site resources in a
limited system over an indefinite interval, in the presence of other
plants."

Prescribed Burning

The lighter fluid for these poems is A.R. Ammons' "The Wind Coming From Down" and "The Wide Land" from *The Selected Poems* (New York: Norton, 1986) p. 10, 13.

Exegesis and Her Song

As the poem indicates, its first stanza is from Czeslaw Milosz's "Over Cities" which is Part III of the title poem in *Bells In Winter*. (New York: Ecco, 1978) p. 50.

How Many Sea Men

This poem relies on the literary work of many others: the epigraph and internal quote in section 3 are from Herman Melville's *Moby Dick* (New York: Norton, 1967) pp. 315, 382. The Gnostic text referred to in section 5 is "The Secret Gospel According to Mark" in *The Other Bible* (San Francisco: Harper & Row). Section 8's "letter after letter that still distinguish us" are from Czeslaw Milosz's "Over Cities" in *Bells In Winter* (New York: Ecco, 1978) p. 50. "Wisdom wisdom" and "unity can not do" are from A.R. Ammons's "Guide" in *The Selected Poems*, Expanded Edition (New York: Norton, 1986) pp. 23-24. "Horror Horror" harkens back to Joseph Conrad's *Heart Of Darkness*. The core of the conclusion cites Eleanor Wilner's title poem "Sarah's Choice" (Chicago: University of Chicago Press, 1989) p. 23.

Grave Stones Dressed

This poem, and others which make reference to stone Isises, are fictions. My wild imagination was triggered by photos in Elizabeth Walters's *Attic Grave Reliefs That Represent Women in the Dress of Isis* (New Jersey: Hesperia, 1988. Supplement XXII.).

ABOUT THE AUTHOR

LORI ANDERSON was born in Central Montana and raised in Northern California. She spent her adolescence training for the 400 meter hurdles and competed nationally. She received undergraduate degrees from Oregon State University where she studied forest management and journalism. After working in Minnesota and Iowa as a farm reporter, she earned an M.F.A. from The Iowa Writers' Workshop at the University of Iowa. For several years she taught at SUNY Cobleskill before returning to school to do graduate work in playwriting, poetry, and ecofeminism. As a student at SUNY Albany, she performs with Archetext—a collaborative of writers and artists presenting their work through dance, music, drama, mixed media and the spoken word. Along with other members of Sisters of Color Writing Collective, she participates in writing workshops that explore racial and cultural diversity. She is on the editorial board of *The Little Magazine* and *Art & Understanding*. Her chapbook, *Walking the Dead*, won the 1990 Heaven Bone Press International Chapbook Competition and was published in 1991. *Cultivating Excess* is her first book.

About the Cover Artist

Angelina C. Marino came to visual art through her work in theater and music. Her preoccupation is with capturing movement and the immediacy of experience. She particularly likes to work in collaboration with artists in other mediums, and is currently at work on a piece that includes dance and poetry. She is self-taught. She lives in Portland, Oregon and her work is shown in various galleries throughout the Northwest. The cover art is soft pastel on black Murillo.

About the Book

Marcia Barrentine designed the cover for *Cultivating Excess*. She is a graphic designer and artist who lives in Portland, Oregon. The text typography was composed in Palatino. The cover typography was composed in Goudy Old Style. The book was printed and bound by Gilliland Printing on acid-free paper. *Cultivating Excess* has been issued in a first edition of two thousand copies of which two hundred fifty are clothbound.

OTHER BOOKS FROM THE
EIGHTH MOUNTAIN PRESS

TRYING TO BE AN HONEST WOMAN
Judith Barrington
1985

COWS AND HORSES
Barbara Wilson
1988

HISTORY AND GEOGRAPHY
Judith Barrington
1989

A FEW WORDS IN THE MOTHER TONGUE
POEMS SELECTED AND NEW (1971–1990)
Irena Klepfisz
Introduction by Adrienne Rich
1990

DREAMS OF AN INSOMNIAC
JEWISH FEMINIST ESSAYS, SPEECHES AND DIATRIBES
Irena Klepfisz
Introduction by Evelyn Torton Beck
1990

INCIDENTS INVOLVING MIRTH
Anna Livia
1990

MINIMAX
Anna Livia
1991

AN INTIMATE WILDERNESS
LESBIAN WRITERS ON SEXUALITY
Judith Barrington, Editor
1991